President Barack Obama signs the Presidential Memorandum establishing the White House Task Force to Protect Students From Sexual Assault on January 22, 2014. (Official White House Photo by Lawrence Jackson)

Sexual violence is more than just a crime against individuals. It threatens our families, it threatens our communities; ultimately, it threatens the entire country. It tears apart the fabric of our communities. And that's why we're here today -- because we have the power to do something about it as a government, as a nation. We have the capacity to stop sexual assault, support those who have survived it, and bring perpetrators to justice.

President Barack Obama, January 22, 2014

Freedom from sexual assault is a basic human right... a nation's decency is in large part measured by how it responds to violence against women... our daughters, our sisters, our wives, our mothers, our grandmothers have every single right to expect to be free from violence and sexual abuse.

Vice President Joe Biden, January 22, 2014

This report was prepared by the White House Task Force to Protect Students From Sexual Assault.

The Task Force is Co-Chaired by the Office of the Vice President and the White House Council on Women and Girls.

Table of Contents

Executive Summary 2

Introduction 6

Our First Task: Listening 6

I. How Best to Identify the Problem: Campus Climate Surveys 7

II. Preventing Sexual Assault on Campus..9

III. Responding Effectively When a Student is Sexually Assaulted 11

IV. Improving the Federal Government's Enforcement Efforts, and
     Making Them More Transparent 16

Next Steps 20

Executive Summary

Why We Need to Act

One in five women is sexually assaulted in college. Most often, it's by someone she knows – and also most often, she does not report what happened. Many survivors are left feeling isolated, ashamed or to blame. Although it happens less often, men, too, are victims of these crimes.

The President created the Task Force to Protect Students From Sexual Assault to turn this tide. As the name of our new website – NotAlone.gov – indicates, we are here to tell sexual assault survivors that they are not alone. And we're also here to help schools live up to their obligation to protect students from sexual violence.

Over the last three months, we have had a national conversation with thousands of people who care about this issue. Today, we offer our first set of action steps and recommendations.

1. Identifying the Problem: Campus Climate Surveys

The first step in solving a problem is to name it and know the extent of it – and a campus climate survey is the best way to do that. We are providing schools with a toolkit to conduct a survey – and we urge schools to show they're serious about the problem by conducting the survey next year. The Justice Department, too, will partner with Rutgers University's Center on Violence Against Women and Children to pilot, evaluate and further refine the survey – and at the end of this trial period, we will explore legislative or administrative options to require schools to conduct a survey in 2016.

2. Preventing Sexual Assault – and Engaging Men

Prevention programs can change attitudes, behavior – and the culture. In addition to identifying a number of promising prevention strategies that schools can undertake now, we are also researching new ideas and solutions. But one thing we know for sure: we need to engage men as allies in this cause. Most men are not perpetrators – and when we empower men to step in when someone's in trouble, they become an important part of the solution.

As the President and Vice President's new Public Service Announcement puts it: if she doesn't consent – or can't consent – it's a crime. And if you see it happening, help her, don't blame her, speak up. We are also providing schools with links and information about how they can implement their own bystander intervention programs on campus.

3. Effectively Responding When a Student Is Sexually Assaulted

When one of its students is sexually assaulted, a school needs to have all the pieces of a plan in place. And that should include:

Someone a survivor can talk to in confidence

While many victims of sexual assault are ready to file a formal (or even public) complaint against an alleged offender right away – many others want time and privacy to sort through their next steps. For some, having a confidential place to go can mean the difference between getting help and staying silent.

Today, we are providing schools with a model reporting and confidentiality protocol – which, at its heart, aims to give survivors more control over the process. Victims who want their school to fully investigate an incident must be taken seriously – and know where to report. But for those who aren't quite ready, they need to have – and know about – places to go for confidential advice and support.

That means a school should make it clear, up front, who on campus can maintain a victim's confidence and who can't – so a victim can make an informed decision about where best to turn. A school's policy should also explain when it may need to override a confidentiality request (and pursue an alleged perpetrator) in order to help provide a safe campus for everyone. Our sample policy provides recommendations for how a school can strike that often difficult balance, while also being ever mindful of a survivor's well-being.

New guidance from the Department of Education also makes clear that on-campus counselors and advocates – like those who work or volunteer in sexual assault centers, victim advocacy offices, women's and health centers, as well as licensed and pastoral counselors – can talk to a survivor in confidence. In recent years, some schools have indicated that some of these counselors and advocates cannot maintain confidentiality. This new guidance clarifies that they can.

A comprehensive sexual misconduct policy

We are also providing a checklist for schools to use in drafting (or reevaluating) their own sexual misconduct policies. Although every school will need to tailor a policy to its own needs and circumstances, all schools should be sure to bring the key stakeholders – including students – to the table. Among other things, this checklist includes ideas a school could consider in deciding what is – or is not – consent to sexual activity. As we heard from many students, this can often be the essence of the matter – and a school community should work together to come up with a careful and considered understanding.

Trauma-informed training for school officials

Sexual assault is a unique crime: unlike other crimes, victims often blame themselves; the associated trauma can leave their memories fragmented; and insensitive or judgmental questions can compound a victim's distress. Starting this year, the Justice Department, through both its Center for Campus Public Safety and its Office on Violence Against Women, will develop trauma-informed training programs for school officials and campus and local law enforcement. The Department of Education's National Center on Safe and Supportive Learning Environments will do the same for campus health centers. This kind of training has multiple benefits: when survivors are treated with care and wisdom, they start trusting the system, and the strength of their accounts can better hold offenders accountable.

Better school disciplinary systems

Many sexual assault survivors are wary of their school's adjudication process – which can sometimes subject them to harsh and hurtful questioning (like about their prior sexual history) by students or staff unschooled in the dynamics of these crimes. Some schools are experimenting with new models – like having a single, trained investigator do the lion's share of the fact-finding – with very positive results. We need to learn more about these promising new ideas. And so starting this year, the Justice Department will begin assessing different models for investigating and adjudicating campus sexual assault cases with an eye toward identifying best practices.

The Department of Education's new guidance also urges some important improvements to many schools' current disciplinary processes: questions about the survivor's sexual history with anyone other than the alleged perpetrator should not be permitted; adjudicators should know that the mere fact of a previous consensual sexual relationship does not itself imply consent or preclude a finding of sexual violence; and the parties should not be allowed to personally cross-examine each other.

Partnerships with the community

Because students can be sexually assaulted at all hours of the day or night, emergency services should be available 24 hours a day, too. Other types of support can also be crucial – like longer-term therapies and advocates who can accompany survivors to medical and legal appointments. Many schools cannot themselves provide all these services, but in partnership with a local rape crisis center, they can. So, too, when both the college and the local police are simultaneously investigating a case (a criminal investigation does not relieve a school of its duty to itself investigate and respond), coordination can be crucial. So we are providing schools with a sample agreement they can use to partner with their local rape crisis center – and by June, we will provide a similar sample for forging a partnership with local law enforcement.

4.   Increasing Transparency and Improving Enforcement

More transparency and information

The government is committed to making our enforcement efforts more transparent – and getting students and schools more resources to help bring an end to this violence. As part of this effort, we will post enforcement data on our new website – NotAlone.gov – and give students a roadmap for filing a complaint if they think their school has not lived up to its obligations.

Among many other things on the website, sexual assault survivors can also locate an array of services by typing in their zip codes, learn about their legal rights, see which colleges have had enforcement actions taken against them, get "plain English" definitions of some complicated legal terms and concepts; and find their states' privacy laws. Schools and advocates can access federal guidance, learn about relevant legislation, and review the best available evidence and research. We invite everyone to take a look.

Improved Enforcement

Today, the Department of Education's Office for Civil Rights (OCR) is releasing a 52-point guidance document that answers many frequently asked questions about a student's rights, and a school's obligations, under Title IX. Among many other topics, the new guidance clarifies that Title IX protects all students, regardless of their sexual orientation or gender identity, immigration status, or whether they have a disability. It also makes clear that students who report sexual violence have a right to expect their school to take steps to protect and support them, including while a school investigation is pending. The guidance also clarifies that recent amendments to the Clery Act do not alter a school's responsibility under Title IX to respond to and prevent sexual violence.

OCR is also strengthening its enforcement procedures in a number of ways – by, for example, instituting time limits on negotiating voluntary resolution agreements and making clear that schools should provide survivors with interim relief (like changing housing or class schedules) pending the outcome of an OCR investigation. And OCR will be more visible on campus during its investigations, so students can help give OCR a fuller picture about what's happening and how a school is responding.

The Departments of Education and Justice, which both enforce Title IX, have entered into an agreement to better coordinate their efforts – as have the two offices within the Department of Education charged with enforcing Title IX and the Clery Act.

Next Steps

This report is the first step in the Task Force's work. We will continue to work toward solutions, clarity, and better coordination. We will also review the various laws and regulations that address sexual violence for possible regulatory or statutory improvements, and seek new resources to enhance enforcement. Also, campus law enforcement officials have special expertise to offer – and they should be tapped to play a more central role. We will also consider how our recommendations apply to public elementary and secondary schools – and what more we can do to help there.

* * *

The Task Force thanks everyone who has offered their wisdom, stories, expertise, and experiences over the past 90 days. Although the problem is daunting and much of what we heard was heartbreaking, we are more committed than ever to helping bring an end to this violence.

Introduction

For too many of our nation's young people, college doesn't turn out the way it's supposed to.

One in five women is sexually assaulted while in college.[1] Most often, it happens her freshman or sophomore year.[2] In the great majority of cases (75-80%), she knows her attacker, whether as an acquaintance, classmate, friend or (ex)boyfriend.[3] Many are survivors of what's called "incapacitated assault": they are sexually abused while drugged, drunk, passed out, or otherwise incapacitated.[4] And although fewer and harder to gauge, college men, too, are victimized.[5]

The Administration is committed to turning this tide. The White House Task Force to Protect Students From Sexual Assault was established on January 22, 2014, with a mandate to strengthen federal enforcement efforts and provide schools with additional tools to help combat sexual assault on their campuses. Today, we are taking a series of initial steps to:

1. **Identify the scope of the problem on college campuses;**
2. **Help prevent campus sexual assault;**
3. **Help schools respond effectively when a student is assaulted; and**
4. **Improve, and make more transparent, the federal government's enforcement efforts.**

As the Task Force recognized at the outset, campus sexual assault is a complicated, multi-dimensional problem with no easy or quick solutions. These initial recommendations do not purport to find or even identify all of them. Our work is not over.[6]

---

[1]   Krebs, C.P., Lindquist, C.H., Warner, T.D., Fisher, B.S., & Martin, S.L. (2007). *The Campus Sexual Assault (CSA) Study*. Washington, DC: National Institute of Justice, U.S. Department of Justice.; Krebs, C.P., Lindquist, C.H., Warner, T.D., Fisher, B.S., & Martin, S.L. (2009). College Women's Experiences with Physically Forced, Alcohol- or Other Drug-Enabled, and Drug-Facilitated Sexual Assault Before and Since Entering College. *Journal of American College Health*, 57(6), 639-647.

[2]   Krebs et al., *The Campus Sexual Assault (CSA) Study.*

[3]   *Ibid.*

[4]   *Ibid.; see also* Kilpatrick, D.G., Resnick, H.S., Ruggiero, K.J., Conoscenti, L.M., & McCauley, J. (2007). *Drug Facilitated, Incapacitated, and Forcible Rape: A National Study*. Charleston, SC: Medical University of South Carolina, National Crime Victims Research & Treatment Center.

[5]   The *CSA Study* found that 6.1% of college males were victims of ether attempted or completed sexual assault. Although many advocates prefer to use the term "survivor" to describe an individual who has been sexually assaulted, the term "victim" is also widely used. This document uses the terms interchangeably and always with respect for those who have been subjected to these crimes.

[6]   This first Task Force report focuses on sexual assault at postsecondary institutions – such as colleges, universities, community colleges, graduate and professional schools, and trade schools – that receive federal financial assistance. Thus, our use of the term "schools" refers to these postsecondary institutions.

Our First Task: Listening

Many people are committed to solving this problem. To hear as many of their views as possible, the Task Force held 27 listening sessions (12 webinars and 15 in-person meetings) with stakeholders from across the country: we heard from survivors; student activists; faculty, staff and administrators from schools of all types; parents; alumni; national survivors' rights and education associations; local and campus-based service providers and advocates; law enforcement; civil rights activists; school general counsels; men's and women's groups; Greek organizations; athletes; and researchers and academics in the field. Thousands of people joined the conversation.

Not surprisingly, no one idea carried the day. But certain common themes did emerge. Many schools are making important strides and are searching in earnest for solutions. A new generation of student activists is effectively pressing for change, asking hard questions, and coming up with innovative ways to make our campuses safer.

Even so, many problems loom large. Prevention and education programs vary widely, with many doing neither well. And in all too many instances, survivors of sexual violence are not at the heart of an institution's response: they often do not have a safe, confidential place to turn after an assault, they haven't been told how the system works, and they often believe it is working against them. We heard from many who reached out for help or action, but were told they should just put the matter behind them.

Schools, for their part, are looking for guidance on their legal obligations and best practices to keep students safe. Many participants called on the federal government to improve and better coordinate our enforcement efforts, and to be more transparent. And there was another constant refrain: get men involved. Most men are not perpetrators – and when we empower men to speak up and intervene when someone's in trouble, they become an important part of the solution.

I. How Best to Identify the Problem: Campus Climate Surveys

When then-Senator Joe Biden wrote the Violence Against Women Act 20 years ago, he recognized a basic truth: no problem can be solved unless we name it and know the extent of it. That is especially true when it comes to campus sexual assault, which is chronically underreported: only 2% of incapacitated sexual assault survivors, and 13% of forcible rape survivors, report the crime to campus or local law enforcement.[7]

The reasons for non-reporting (whether to a school or to law enforcement) vary. Many survivors of acquaintance rape don't call what happened to them rape and often blame themselves. One report found that 40% of college survivors feared reprisal by the perpetrator.[8] Survivors also cite

---

[7] Krebs et al., *The Campus Sexual Assault (CSA) Study.*
[8] Sampson, Rana (2002). *Acquaintance Rape of College Students*; Washington, DC: Office of Community Oriented Policing Services, U.S. Department of Justice.

fear of treatment by authorities, not knowing how to report, lack of independent proof, and not wanting families or other students to find out what happened.[9] Still others don't report because they don't want to participate in a formal college adjudication process.[10]

For colleges and universities, breaking the cycle of violence poses a unique challenge. When a school tries to tackle the problem – by acknowledging it, drawing attention to it, and encouraging survivors to report – it can start to look like a dangerous place. On the flip side, when a school ignores the problem or discourages reporting (either actively or by treating survivors without care), it can look safer. Add to this the competition for top students or a coveted spot on a college rankings list – and a school might think it can outshine its neighbor by keeping its problem in the shadows.

We have to change that dynamic.

Schools have to get credit for being honest – and for finding out what's really happening on campus. Reports to authorities, as we know, don't provide a fair measure of the problem. But a campus climate survey can. When done right, these surveys can gauge the prevalence of sexual assault on campus, test students' attitudes and awareness about the issue, and provide schools with an invaluable tool for crafting solutions. And so:

- **We are providing schools with a new toolkit for developing and conducting a climate survey**. This guide explains the methods for conducting an effective survey – and contains a set of evidence-based sample questions to get at the answers.

- **We call on colleges and universities to voluntarily conduct the survey next year.** Again, a school that is willing to get an accurate assessment of sexual assault on its campus is one that's taking the problem – and the solution – seriously. Researchers recommend that schools conduct the survey in the winter or spring semesters, rather than when students first arrive on campus in the fall.

  Rutgers University, with its leading research institute on violence against women,[11] will pilot and evaluate the survey. Also, the Justice Department's Office on Violence Against Women will work with its campus grantees to conduct the survey and evaluate it. And the Bureau of Justice Statistics will further refine the survey methodology.
  What we learn from these pilots, evaluations, and schools' experiences will chart the path forward for everyone – and will culminate in a survey for all to use.

- **We will explore legislative or administrative options to require colleges and universities to conduct an evidence-based survey in 2016.** A mandate for schools to periodically conduct a climate survey will change the national dynamic: with a better picture of what's really happening on campus, schools will be able to more effectively tackle the problem and measure the success of their efforts.

---

[9] Krebs et al., *The Campus Sexual Assault (CSA) Study*.
[10] *Ibid.*
[11] The Center on Violence Against Women & Children at the School of Social Work.

II. Preventing Sexual Assault on Campus

Participants in our listening sessions roundly urged the Task Force to make prevention a top priority. Some even suggested that if prevention and education efforts don't start earlier, it's too late by the time students get to college. While we certainly agree that this work should begin early, the college years, too, are formative. During this transition to adulthood, attitudes and behaviors are created or reinforced by peer groups. And students look to coaches, professors, administrators, and other campus leaders to set the tone. If we get this right, today's students will leave college knowing that sexual assault is simply unacceptable. And that, in itself, can create a sea change.

Federal law now requires schools to provide sexual assault prevention and awareness programs.[12] To help colleges and universities in this endeavor, we are providing schools with new guidance and tools.

- **Best practices for better prevention.** The Centers for Disease Control and Prevention (CDC) conducted a systematic review of primary prevention strategies for reducing sexual violence, and is releasing an advance summary of its findings. CDC's review summarizes some of the best available research in the area, and highlights evidence-based prevention strategies that work, some that are promising, and – importantly – those that don't work. The report points to steps colleges can take now to prevent sexual assault on their campuses.

  Among other things, CDC's review shows that effective programs are those that are sustained (not brief, one-shot educational programs), comprehensive, and address the root individual, relational and societal causes of sexual assault. It also includes a listing of prevention programs being used by colleges and universities across the country, so schools can better compare notes about effective and encouraging approaches.[13]

- **Getting everyone to step in: bystander intervention.** Among the most promising prevention strategies – and one we heard a lot about in our listening sessions – is bystander intervention. Social norms research reveals that men often misperceive what other men think about this issue: they overestimate their peers' acceptance of sexual assault and underestimate other men's willingness to intervene when a woman is in trouble.[14] And when men think their peers don't object to abusive behavior, they are

---

[12]   *See* 20 U.S.C. § 1092(f) (The Jeanne Clery Disclosure of Campus Security and Campus Crimes Statistics Act, commonly known as the Clery Act). The Department of Education is currently engaged in negotiated rule-making to implement the VAWA 2013 amendments to the Clery Act that require schools to provide education and awareness programs and to improve their campus security policies. Rule-making is scheduled to be completed in 2015, but schools are expected to make a good faith effort now to meet the new requirements.

[13]   For a concise and complementary factsheet on prevention strategies, *see* http://notalone.gov/assets/prevention-overview.pdf.

[14]   Berkowitz, A.D. (2010) "Fostering Healthy Norms to Prevent Violence and Abuse: The Social Norms Approach." Accessed from: http://www.alanberkowitz.com/articles/Preventing%20Sexual%20Violence%20Chapter%20-%20Revision.pdf

much less likely to step in and help. Programs like *Bringing in the Bystander*[15] work to change those perspectives – and teach men (and women) to speak out against rape myths (*e.g.*, women who drink at parties are "asking for it") and to intervene if someone is at risk of being assaulted.

- o **To help enlist men as allies, we are releasing <u>a Public Service Announcement</u> featuring President Obama, Vice President Biden, and celebrity actors.** The message of the PSA is simple: if she doesn't consent – or can't consent – it's a crime. And if you see it happening, help her, don't blame her, speak up. We particularly urge men's groups, Greek organizations, coaches, alumni associations, school officials and other leaders to use the PSA to start campus conversations about sexual assault.

- o **To help keep these conversations going, we are <u>providing a basic factsheet on bystander intervention</u>.** In addition to the CDC summary, this document identifies the messages and skills that effective programs impart, describes the various ways to get the word out (in-person workshops, social marketing campaigns, online training, interactive theater) and provides links to some of the more promising programs out there.

- • **Developing new prevention strategies.** More research is needed to develop and evaluate evidence-based programming to prevent sexual violence on campus. And so:

  - o In Fall 2014, the CDC, in collaboration with the Justice Department's Office on Violence Against Women and the Department of Education, will convene a panel of experts to identify emerging, promising practices to prevent sexual assault on campus. CDC will then convene pilot teams to put the consensus recommendations into practice.

  - o The Justice Department's Office on Violence Against Women (OVW) is developing a multi-year initiative on campus sexual assault which, among other things, will test and evaluate prevention programs used by its campus grantees. Grantees will work with OVW and technical assistance experts to meet core standards and evaluate the results. The next group of campus grantees will be selected by October 2014.

  - o In 2015, the CDC will solicit proposals to identify, and fill, gaps in the research on sexual violence prevention.

---

[15]   Banyard, V. L., Moynihan, M. M., & Plante, E. G. (2007). Sexual violence prevention through bystander education: An experimental evaluation. *Journal of Community Psychology*, 35, 463-481

III. Responding Effectively When a Student is Sexually Assaulted

Sexual assault is a crime – and while some survivors turn to the criminal justice system, others look to their schools for help or recourse. Under federal law, when a school knows or reasonably should know that one of its students has been sexually assaulted, it is obligated to act. These two systems serve different (though often overlapping) goals. The principal aim of the criminal system is to adjudicate a defendant's guilt and serve justice. A school's responsibility is broader: it is charged with providing a safe learning environment for all its students – and to give survivors the help they need to reclaim their educations. And that can mean a number of things – from giving a victim a confidential place to turn for advice and support, to effectively investigating and finding out what happened, to sanctioning the perpetrator, to doing everything we can to help a survivor recover. The Task Force is taking the following steps:

Giving Survivors More Control: Reporting and Confidentially Disclosing What Happened

Sexual assault survivors respond in different ways. Some are ready to make a formal complaint right away, and want their school to move swiftly to hold the perpetrator accountable.

Others, however, aren't so sure. Sexual assault can leave victims feeling powerless – and they need support from the beginning to regain a sense of control. Some, at least at first, don't want their assailant (or the assailant's friends, classmates, teammates or club members) to know they've reported what happened. But they do want someone on campus to talk to – and many want to talk in confidence, so they can sort through their options at their own pace. If victims don't have a confidential place to go, or think a school will launch a full-scale investigation against their wishes, many will stay silent.

In recent years, some schools have directed nearly all their employees (including those who typically offer confidential services, like rape crisis and women's centers) to report all the details of an incident to school officials – which can mean that a survivor quickly loses control over what happens next. That practice, however well-intentioned, leaves survivors with fewer places to turn.

This is, by far, the problem we heard most about in our listening sessions. To help solve it:

- **Schools should identify trained, confidential victim advocates who can provide emergency and ongoing support.** This is a key "best practice." The person a victim talks to first is often the most important. This person should understand the dynamics of sexual assault and the unique toll it can take on self-blaming or traumatized victims. The advocate should also be able to help get a victim needed resources and accommodations, explain how the school's grievance and disciplinary system works, and help navigate the process. As many advocates have learned over the years, after survivors receive initial, confidential support, they often decide to proceed with a formal complaint or cooperate in an investigation.

- **We are also providing schools with <u>a sample reporting and confidentiality protocol</u>.** A school, of course, must make any policy its own – but a few guiding principles should universally apply. As noted, some sexual assault survivors are ready to press forward with a formal (or even public) complaint, while others need time and privacy to heal. There is no one-size-fits-all model of victim care. Instead, there must be options.

  That means, at a minimum, that schools should make it clear, up front, who on campus will (or will not) share what information with whom. And a school's policy should also explain when it may need to override a request for confidentiality (and pursue an alleged perpetrator) in order to provide a safe campus for everyone. The watchword here is clarity: both confidential resources and formal reporting options should be well and widely publicized – so a victim can make an informed decision about where best to turn.

  And in all cases, the school must respond. When a student wants the school to take action against an offender – or to change dorms or working arrangements – the school must take the allegation seriously, and not dissuade a report or otherwise keep the survivor's story under wraps. Where a survivor does not seek a full investigation, but just wants help to move on, the school needs to respond there, too. And because a school has a continuing obligation to address sexual violence campus-wide, it should always think about broader remedial action – like increasing education and prevention efforts (including to targeted groups), boosting security and surveillance at places where students have been sexually assaulted, and/or revisiting its policies and practices.

Developing a Comprehensive Sexual Misconduct Policy

Every college and university should have an easily accessible, user-friendly sexual misconduct policy. As the Task Force recognizes, there is no one approach that suits every school – but as we also learned, many schools don't have adequate policies. To help:

- **We are providing schools with <u>a checklist for a sexual misconduct policy</u>.** This checklist provides both a suggested process for developing a policy, as well as the key elements a school should consider in drafting one. Importantly, schools should bring all the key stakeholders to the table – including students, survivors, campus security, law enforcement, resident advisors, student groups (including LGBTQ groups), on-campus advocates, and local victim service providers. Effective policies will vary in scope and detail, but an inclusive process is common to all.

  We have not endeavored with this checklist to provide schools with all the answers: again, depending on its size, mission, student body, location, administrative structure and experience, a school community needs to tailor the checklist and make the policy its own.

- **By September 2014, the Task Force will provide samples of promising policy language on several other key issues.** While all schools are different, we have identified several challenging areas (in addition to confidentiality) where sample language could be helpful. These include definitions of various forms of sexual misconduct; the role of the

Title IX coordinator (recognizing that there may be various appropriate models for different schools); and the proper immediate, interim and long-term measures a school should take on behalf of survivors, whether or not they seek a full investigation.

Training for School Officials

Sexual assault can be hard to understand. Some common victim responses (like not physically resisting or yelling for help) may seem counter-intuitive to those unfamiliar with sexual victimization. New research has also found that the trauma associated with rape or sexual assault can interfere with parts of the brain that control memory – and, as a result, a victim may have impaired verbal skills, short term memory loss, memory fragmentation, and delayed recall.[16] This can make understanding what happened challenging.

Personal biases also come into play. Insensitive or judgmental comments – or questions that focus on a victim's behavior (*e.g.*, what she was wearing, her prior sexual history) rather than on the alleged perpetrator's – can compound a victim's distress.

Specialized training, thus, is crucial. School officials and investigators need to understand how sexual assault occurs, how it's perpetrated, and how victims might naturally respond both during and after an assault. To help:

- **By September 2014, the Justice Department's Center for Campus Public Safety will develop a training program for campus officials involved in investigating and adjudicating sexual assault cases.** The Clery Act requires these officials to receive annual training on sexual assault (and also on domestic violence, dating violence and stalking). The Center will develop a trauma-informed training program consistent with the new requirements.

- **By June 2014, the Justice Department's Office on Violence Against Women will launch a comprehensive online technical assistance project for campus officials.** Key topics will include victim services, coordinated community responses, alcohol and drug-facilitated sexual assaults, and Clery Act compliance. Webinars and materials will include the latest research, promising practices, training opportunities, policy updates, prevention programming, and recent publications. The project will feature strategies and training materials for campus and local law enforcement.

- **By December 2014, the Department of Education, through the National Center on Safe and Supportive Learning Environments, will develop trauma-informed training materials for campus health center staff.** Often, campus health centers are the first responders for victims of sexual assault. Services will vary according to the

---

[16] Bremner, J.D., Elzinga, B., Schmahl, C., & Vermetten, E. (2008). Structural and functional plasticity of the human brain in posttraumatic stress disorder. *Progress in Brain Research*. *167*(1), 171-186; Nixon, R. D., Nishith, P., & Resick, P. A. (2004). The Accumulative Effect of Trauma Exposure on Short-Term and Delayed Verbal Memory in a Treatment-Seeking Sample of Female Rape Victims. *Journal of Traumatic Stress*, *17*(1), 31-35.

school's resources, but all staff should be trained on trauma-informed care – and these materials will help.

New Investigative and Adjudicative Protocols: Better Holding Offenders Accountable

Separate and apart from training, we also need to know more about what investigative and adjudicative *systems* work best on campus: that is, who should gather the evidence; who should make the determination whether a sexual assault occurred; who should decide the sanction; and what an appeals process, if the school has one, should look like.

Schools are experimenting with new ideas. Some are adopting different variations on the "single investigator" model, where a trained investigator or investigators interview the complainant and alleged perpetrator, gather any physical evidence, interview available witnesses – and then either render a finding, present a recommendation, or even work out an acceptance-of-responsibility agreement with the offender. These models stand in contrast to the more traditional system, where a college hearing or judicial board hears a case (sometimes tracking the adversarial, evidence-gathering criminal justice model), makes a finding, and decides the sanction.

Preliminary reports from the field suggest that these innovative models, in which college judicial boards play a much more limited role, encourage reporting and bolster trust in the process, while at the same time safeguarding an alleged perpetrator's right to notice and to be heard. To evaluate these ideas:

- **By October 2014, the Justice Department's Office on Violence Against Women and National Institute of Justice will begin assessing models for investigating and adjudicating campus sexual assault cases, and identify promising practices.** OVW will also further test and evaluate these models through its campus grantees – which will be selected by October 2014.

- **On April 29, 2014, the Justice Department's SMART Office will release a solicitation for a pilot sex offender treatment program targeting college perpetrators.** Research suggests that treatment can be effective in reducing recidivism among offenders, yet no programs currently exist for the college population. Regardless of campus-imposed sanctions, we need to help reduce the risk that young perpetrators will offend again. This first-of-its kind pilot project holds out new hope for reducing sexual violence on campuses.

Providing Comprehensive Support: Partnering with the Community

Rape Crisis Centers. Sexual assault survivors often need a variety of services, both immediate and long-term, to help them regain a sense of control and safety. While some schools may be able to provide comprehensive trauma-informed services on campus, others may need to partner with community-based organizations.

Regardless of where they are provided, certain key elements should be part of a comprehensive victim-services plan. Because students can be assaulted at all hours of the day or night, crisis intervention services should be available 24 hours a day, too. Survivors also need advocates who can accompany them to medical and legal appointments. And because, for some survivors, the road to recovery is neither short nor easy, longer-term clinical therapies can be crucial.

Rape crisis centers can help schools better serve their students. These centers often provide crisis intervention, 24-hour services, longer-term therapy, support groups, accompaniment to appointments, and community education. Rape crisis centers can also help schools train students and employees and assist in developing prevention programs. And so:

- **To help schools build these partnerships, we are** providing a sample Memorandum of Understanding (MOU) **with a local rape crisis center.** Schools can adapt this MOU depending on their specific needs and the capacity of a local center.

- **To help schools develop or strengthen on-campus programs, we are also** providing a summary of promising practices in victim services. This guide reviews the existing research on sexual assault services and outlines the elements of an effective victim services program.

- **To assist Tribal Colleges and Universities (TCUs) with victim services, the Justice Department's Office on Violence Against Women will continue to prioritize TCUs in its campus grant program solicitations.** OVW is working to raise awareness of funding opportunities by engaging with leading tribal organizations and partnering with the White House Initiative on American Indian and Alaska Native Education. OVW will also work with tribal domestic violence and sexual assault coalitions to provide TCUs with technical assistance on victim services.

Local Law Enforcement. At first blush, many may ask why all cases of sexual assault are not referred to the local prosecutor for criminal prosecution. Some, of course, are – but for many survivors, the criminal process simply does not provide the services and assistance they need to get on with their lives or to get their educations back on track. There are times, however, when the local police and a school may be simultaneously pursuing a case. A criminal investigation does not relieve a school of its independent obligation to conduct its own investigation – nor may a school wait for a criminal case to conclude to proceed. Cooperation in these situations, thus, is critical. So:

- **By June 2014, we will provide schools with a sample Memorandum of Understanding (MOU) with local law enforcement.** An MOU can help open lines of communication and increase coordination among campus security, local law enforcement and other community groups that provide victim services. An MOU can also improve security on and around campus, make investigations and prosecutions more efficient, and increase officers' understanding of the unique needs of sexual assault victims.

Many schools have research institutes that can measurably improve our thinking about sexual assault. Schools are uniquely suited to identify gaps in the research and develop methods to address them. To lead by example, three universities have committed to developing research projects that will better inform their response to the problem and contribute to the national body of work on campus sexual assault:

- The Johns Hopkins University School of Nursing will study sexual assault among student intimate partners, including LGBTQ relationships.

- The University of Texas at Austin School of Social Work will develop and evaluate training for campus law enforcement and examine the effectiveness of Sexual Assault Response Teams.

- The University of New Hampshire Prevention Innovations Center will design and evaluate a training program for incoming students on sexual assault policies and expectations for student conduct.

We invite others to join this collaborative – and to add their own research brains and resources toward finding solutions.

IV. Improving the Federal Government's Enforcement Efforts, and Making Them More Transparent

The federal government plays an important role in combatting sexual violence. And as we outlined in our recent report, "Rape and Sexual Assault: A Renewed Call to Action," this Administration has taken aggressive action on many fronts.

We need to build on these efforts. To better address sexual assault at our nation's schools, we need to both strengthen our enforcement efforts and increase coordination among responsible federal agencies. Also, and importantly, we need to improve our communication with students, parents, school administrators, faculty, and the public, by making our efforts more transparent.

Some Background on the Laws

Title IX of the Education Amendments of 1972, 20 U.S.C. § 1681 *et seq.*, requires schools that receive federal financial assistance to take necessary steps to prevent sexual assault on their campuses, and to respond promptly and effectively when an assault is reported. Title IV of the 1964 Civil Rights Act, 42 U.S.C. § 2000c *et seq.*, also requires public schools to respond to sexual assaults committed against their students. The Clery Act requires colleges and universities that participate in federal financial aid programs to report annual statistics on crime, including sexual assault and rape, on or near their campuses, and to develop and disseminate prevention policies.[17]

The Department of Education's Office for Civil Rights (OCR) is charged with administrative enforcement of Title IX in schools receiving financial assistance from the Department. OCR may initiate an investigation either proactively or in response to a formal complaint. If OCR finds a Title IX violation, the school risks losing federal funds. In these cases, OCR must first seek to voluntarily resolve the non-compliance before terminating funds. Through this voluntary resolution process, OCR has entered into agreements that require schools to take a number of comprehensive steps to remedy the problem on their campuses.

The Department of Education's Federal Student Aid (FSA) office is responsible for enforcing the Clery Act, and conducts on-site reviews to ensure compliance. If a school is found to have violated Clery, FSA directs it to take steps to comply and can impose fines for violations.

The Justice Department (DOJ) is responsible for coordinating enforcement of Title IX across all federal agencies. DOJ shares authority with OCR for enforcing Title IX, and may initiate an investigation or compliance review of schools receiving DOJ financial assistance. If schools are found to violate Title IX and a voluntary resolution cannot be reached, DOJ can initiate litigation, including upon referral from other federal agencies, or seek to terminate DOJ funds. DOJ is also responsible for enforcing Title IV. DOJ can use its authority under Title IV, Title IX, and other federal civil rights statutes to bring all facets of a school, including its campus police, and local police departments into compliance with the law. DOJ can also intervene, file amicus briefs, and/or file statements of interest in court cases involving these statutes.

Improving Transparency and Information-sharing

The Administration is committed to making our enforcement efforts more transparent, and getting schools and students more resources. And so:

- **The Task Force is launching a dedicated website – <u>NotAlone.gov</u> – to make enforcement data public and to make other resources accessible to students and schools.** Although many tools and resources exist, students and schools often haven't been able to access them – either because the materials haven't been widely available or because they are too hard to find. Today, we are changing that.

  Our new website will give students a clear explanation of their rights under Title IX and Title IV, along with a simple description of how to file a complaint with OCR and DOJ and what they should expect throughout the process. It will help students wade through often complicated legal definitions and concepts, and point them toward people who can give them confidential advice – and those who can't.

---

[17]   Other laws also authorize the Justice Department to investigate campus sexual assaults and help campus police as well as local, tribal and state law enforcement adopt comprehensive policies and practices to address the problem. These include the Violent Crime Control and Law Enforcement Act of 1994, 42 U.S.C. § 14141; and the Omnibus Crime Control and Safe Streets Act of 1968, 42 U.S.C. § 3789d.

The website will also put in one central place OCR resolution letters and agreements (except those that raise individual privacy concerns), and all DOJ federal court filings, including complaints, motions, and briefs, consent decrees, and out-of-court agreements (which are also available on DOJ's website). These documents will be posted as a matter of course, so students, school officials, and other stakeholders can easily access the most current agreements.

The website will also contain the relevant guidance on a school's federal obligations, best available evidence and research on prevention programs, and sample policies and model agreements.

Finally, the website will have trustworthy resources from outside the government – like hotline numbers and mental health services locatable by simply typing in a zip code. It will also have a list of resources broken down by issue – like advocacy/survivor services, student groups, or LGBTQ resources – so someone can find more issue-specific information.

- **The Task Force will continue to work with developers and advocates to find ways that tech innovations can help end the violence.** On April 11, more than 60 innovators, technologists, students, policy experts, and survivors of sexual assault gathered at the White House for a "Data Jam" to brainstorm new ways to use technology to shed light on campus sexual assault and better support survivors.

- **Federal agencies are making datasets relevant to sexual assault readily available.** In keeping with the Administration's open data pledge, federal agencies, including the Departments of Education, Justice, Interior, and Health & Human Services have made public more than 100 datasets related to sexual assault and higher education. These datasets include survey results related to sexual violence, program evaluations, and guidance documents. This data is posted on data.gov.

- **The Department of Education is taking additional steps to make its activities more transparent.** As noted, OCR is posting nearly all recent resolution letters and agreements with schools on its website. OCR will also make public the schools that are under OCR investigation, including those that involve Title IX sexual violence allegations. This information will be made available by contacting the Department of Education.

- **The Department of Education will collect and disseminate a list of Title IX coordinators by next year.** Every school must designate at least one employee to coordinate its efforts to carry out its Title IX responsibilities. Although schools must notify students of the name and contact information of the Title IX coordinator, there is no central, national repository of coordinator contact information. The Department of Education's Office of Postsecondary Education and OCR will collect and disseminate the list of higher education Title IX coordinators annually so anyone can easily locate a coordinator. This information will also encourage coordinators to talk to each other and share positive practices to Title IX compliance.

The Administration is also committed to improving, and better coordinating, our enforcement efforts. And so:

- **The Department of Education is providing more clarity on schools' obligations under Title IX.** In April 2011, OCR issued groundbreaking guidance to schools on their obligations to prevent and respond to sexual violence under Title IX. Since then, schools and students have asked for further guidance and clarity – and, today, OCR is issuing its answers to these frequently asked questions.

  Among many other topics, this new guidance clarifies that:

  - Title IX protects all students, regardless of their sexual orientation or gender identity, immigration status, or whether they have a disability;
  - non-professional on-campus counselors and advocates – like those who work or volunteer in on-campus sexual assault centers, victim advocacy offices, women's centers and health centers – can generally talk to a survivor in confidence;
  - questioning or evidence about the survivor's sexual history with anyone other than the alleged perpetrator should not be permitted during a judicial hearing;
  - adjudicators should know that the mere fact of a previous consensual dating or sexual relationship does not itself imply consent or preclude a finding of sexual violence; and
  - the parties should not be allowed to personally cross-examine each other.

  The Q&A also discusses (again, among many other topics) college employees' reporting obligations; the role of the Title IX coordinator; how a school should conduct investigations; and Title IX training, education and prevention.

- **The Department of Education is strengthening its enforcement procedures.** OCR has made changes to its enforcement procedures.[18]

  Among other things, OCR is instituting time limits for negotiating voluntary resolution agreements. By law, OCR is required to pursue a voluntary resolution with a school before initiating an enforcement action. Although this process is usually much faster than litigation, it can also take time and, as a result, be frustrating for survivors who typically remain on campus or enrolled in school for a limited time. To help guard against the risk that a school may extend negotiations to delay enforcement, OCR is placing a 90-day limit on voluntary resolution agreement negotiations where it has found a school in violation of Title IX.

  OCR's procedures also now make explicit that schools should provide survivors with interim relief – such as changing housing or class schedules, issuing no-contact orders, or providing counseling – pending the outcome of an OCR investigation. OCR will also be

---

[18] *See* http://www2.ed.gov/about/offices/list/ocr/docs/ocrcpm.html.

more visible on campus and reach out to more students and school officials during its investigations, in order to get a fuller picture as to whether or not there is a problem on campus.

- **The Department of Education is also clarifying how key federal laws intersect.** In addition to Title IX and the Clery Act, the Family Educational Rights and Privacy Act (FERPA),[19] which protects the privacy of student education records, can also come into play in campus sexual violence investigations. In response to requests for guidance, the Department of Education has created a chart outlining a school's reporting obligations under Title IX and the Clery Act, and how each intersects with FERPA. The chart shows that although the requirements of Title IX and the Clery Act may differ in some ways, they don't conflict.

- **The Departments of Education and Justice have entered into an agreement clarifying each agency's role vis-à-vis Title IX.** OCR and the Justice Department's Civil Rights Division (CRT) both enforce Title IX. To increase coordination and strengthen enforcement, the agencies have entered into a formal memorandum of understanding.[20]

- **The Department of Education offices responsible for Title IX and Clery Act enforcement have also entered into an agreement clarifying their respective roles.** As noted, the Federal Student Aid (FSA) office is responsible for Clery Act compliance, whereas OCR enforces Title IX. Sometimes, their efforts overlap. To clarify their roles and increase efficiency, FSA and OCR have formalized an agreement to ensure more efficient and effective handling of complaints and to facilitate information sharing.

Next Steps

The action steps and recommendations highlighted in this report are the initial phase of an ongoing plan. The Task Force is mindful, for instance, of the continuing challenges schools face in meeting Title IX and Clery Act requirements. We will continue to work toward solutions, clarity, and better coordination. We will also review the various laws and regulations that address sexual violence for possible regulatory or statutory improvements, and seek new resources to enhance enforcement. Also, campus law enforcement officials have special expertise – and they should be tapped to play a more central role. We will also consider how our recommendations apply to public elementary and secondary schools – and what more we can do to help there.

Our work continues.

---

[19] 20 U.S.C. § 1232g; 34 C.F.R. Part 99.
[20] *See* http://www.justice.gov/crt/about/cor/ED_DOJ_MOU_TitleIX-04-29-2014.pdf.